CONTENTS

The team game

Football is an action-packed team sport that pits two sides, each containing 11 players, against each other. The players control, pass and run with the ball with the aim of scoring goals.

Working together

Throughout the world of football, there are plenty of cases of players from supposedly weaker sides using good tactics and working well together to beat teams full of superstars. For example, even though the England team consisted of many superstar players, such as Steven Gerrard, they lost games and failed to qualify for the Euro 2008 tournament. There are plenty of examples of sides beaten by supposedly lesser teams – a feat known as giant-killing. In Euro 2004, nobody thought Greece would win, but by working together, the team lifted the trophy after beating Portugal, Spain and France along the way.

Spain's superstar players celebrate winning Euro 2008. With further good tactics and teamwork, they went on to win the 2010 World Cup as well.

FOOTBALL FOCUS

TEAMWORK AND TACTICS

TOWER HAMLETS COLLEGE
POPLAR HIGH STREET
LONDON
E14 OAF

Clive Gifford

WAYLAND

Prinred in 2012

Wayland
338 Euston Road
London NW1 3BH

Wayland Australia
Level 17/207 Kent Street
Sydney, NSW 2000

Editor: Julia Adams
Produced by Tall Tree Ltd
Editor, Tall Tree: Jon Richards
Designer: Ben Ruocco

British Library Cataloguing in Publication Data

Gifford, Clive.
   Teamwork and tactics. -- (Football focus)
   1. Soccer--Juvenile literature. 2. Teamwork
(Sports)--Juvenile literature.
   I. Title II. Series
   796.3'342-dc22

ISBN 9780750267526

Printed in China

Wayland is a division of Hachette Children's Books,
an Hachette UK company.

www.hachette.co.uk

First published in 2009 by Wayland

This paperback edition published by Wayland in 2012

Reprinted in 2012

Acknowledgements
The author and publisher would like to thank the
following people for their help and participation in this
book: Whiteknights FC, Eric Burrow, Steve Rendell and
Paul Scholey

Picture credits
All photographs taken by Michael Wicks, except;
t - top, l - left, r - right, b - bottom, c - centre
cover t - Dreamstime.com/Val_th, tr - Dreamstime.com/
Sebcz, br - Dreamstime.com/Val_th, bl - Dreamstime.
com/Spartak, tl - Michael Wicks, c - Dreamstime.
com/Katseyephoto, 2 Dreamstime.com/Mitchell
Gunn, 4 Andres Kudacki/Corbis, 8 Dreamstime.com/
Mitchell Gunn, 16 Gilbert Iundt/TempSport/Corbis,
17b Dreamstime.com/Mitchell Gunn, 24 Greg Fiume/
NewSport/Corbis, 25 Dreamstime.com/Susana Carvalho,
26br Getty Images, 27 Sampics/Corbis, 30 Ben Radford/
Corbis, 32 Dreamstime.com/Susana Carvalho

The website addresses (URLs) included in this book were
valid at the time of going to press. However, because
of the nature of the Internet, it is possible that some
addresses may have changed, or sites may have changed
or closed down since publication. While the author and
Publisher regret any inconvenience this may cause the
readers, no responsibility for any such changes can be
accepted by either the author or the Publisher.

Disclaimer
In preparation of this book, all due care has been
exercised with regard to the advice, activities and
techniques depicted. The publishers regret that they can
accept no liability for any loss or injury sustained. When
learning a new sport it is important to get expert tuition
and to follow a manufacturer's instructions.

Plenty of practice in small five-a-side games will help to improve teamwork and coordination and turn a group of individuals into a well-organised unit.

Individuals and teams

While players need excellent individual skills, football is a team game. The media (newspapers, television, radio and the Internet) often focus on a star individual in a side, such as the team's most skilful winger or its most successful goalscorer. These players may be game changers, but without the support and good play of the rest of their side, they are unlikely to shine. How a team is organised and how the players choose to attack and defend are known as tactics. These are usually decided on by the team's coach or manager.

> *I've never considered one player to be all-important. In football you win or lose together as a team.*
>
> Italian striker
> **Alessandro Del Piero**

Training and the team

Working well as a team takes hours of training. While training is essential to improve each footballer's own skills, it is also where players get to know each other's strengths and weaknesses.

Types of training

Players train regularly, beginning with a warm-up and a series of muscle stretches. They then take part in a series of drills and games designed to sharpen their speed, skills and awareness. All the time, the players learn more about how their team-mates run, which foot they prefer to use and how good they are at heading the ball. Teams often play a lot of training games, such as five-a-side. These games help players communicate with each other and build partnerships on the pitch.

Tactics Tip

Do not try to hurry your warm-up. Take your time to stretch your muscles and build up your heart rate steadily. If you try to do too much too quickly you could injure yourself.

Warming up

1 Warming up should start with gentle jogging. This raises the players' heart rate and gradually warms up their muscles.

2 Jogging should be followed by gentle stretching. Here, the players are stretching the hamstring muscles at the backs of their legs.

3 After stretching, players can start some more strenuous exercise to raise the heart rate even more, such as sprints as these players are doing.

Watching players

Coaches watch training closely. How the players train can have a major influence on who the coaches select to play and what tactics they choose for their teams. For example, a star player may look tired in training and this might force the coach to not play them in the next match or to put them on the substitute's bench. The coach may also discover that someone is capable of playing in more than one position. If the team is hit by injuries, the coach may try this player out in a new position.

Failure happens all the time. It happens every day in practice. What makes you better is how you react to it.

United States women's team record goalscorer **Mia Hamm**

These players are taking part in a simple training routine called a one-touch triangle. They stand in a triangle and pass the ball quickly between each other using just one touch. This helps the players develop their passing skills with both feet and it also helps their team-mates spot which foot they favour.

Decision makers

Coaches and managers are the people in charge of football teams. Managers are involved in some of the business of a club, such as buying and selling players. Coaches are involved just in training players for the matches.

Making decisions

Coaches and managers have a squad of players from which they can select a team to start a match. They will base their decisions on the tactics they want to use and the strengths of their available players. Sometimes, a coach or manager will risk the anger of fans to drop a star player who is tired or playing badly. Spanish coach José Luis Aragones did not take striker Raul to Euro 2008, a move which outraged some fans. However, Spain went on to win the competition.

Sir Alex Ferguson is one of the most successful managers in the world. In more than 20 years in charge at Manchester United, he has won 12 Premier League titles and two Champions League crowns.

Pre-match briefing

Players discuss tactics and listen to their coach's briefing before a match. This is when the coach tells his players what tactics they should use during the game. However, there should be another plan if the original one does not work.

Tactics Tip

Listen carefully to your coach's pre-match briefing, but do not be afraid to say if the plan is not working during a match. Sometimes, the players are better placed to see what is happening on the pitch.

Scouting opponents

At the top level, coaches and managers study their upcoming opponents carefully. They attend matches, send assistants to scout the opponents and watch recorded matches on computers or DVD. All the time, they are looking for weaknesses and how their own team might exploit them. At the 2010 FIFA World Cup, Germany's coach Joachim Löw used tactics to stretch the English defence and get his fast-moving attackers in on goal. Germany recorded a famous 4-1 victory, knocking England out of the World Cup.

Formations

Teams are made up of a goalkeeper and three basic types of outfield player called defenders, midfielders and strikers or attackers. How these players line up to start a game is called a team's formation.

A wing back (in blue) surges forwards with the ball at his feet to start an attack. Wing backs play mainly along the flanks of the pitch.

> *Good players win you games, good formations stop you losing them.*
>
> Former Celtic manager, **Gordon Strachan**

Playing positions

Defenders are responsible for stopping the opposition scoring goals. They tend to be good at heading the ball away and strong in the tackle. Full backs are defenders who play closer to the sidelines. Midfielders help in both defence and attack. They cover a lot of ground during a game. Midfielders who play out near the sidelines are known as wingers. These are attack-minded players whose aim is to beat defenders and shoot or pass to a team-mate. Teams play with one, two or, occasionally, three strikers. These are a side's strongest goalscorers and tend to play closest to the opponent's goal.

Team structure

Playing formations are expressed as numbers in rows of defenders, midfielders and attackers. For example, a 4-4-2 formation means four defenders, four midfielders and two strikers. Formations can be more complicated with one footballer playing behind a single striker (4-4-1-1), or a midfield anchor playing just in front of the defence (4-1-3-2). Another popular formation today is 3-5-2, with the two players, called wing backs, on the flanks of the five-man midfield.

ON THE BALL

In 1872, England used a 1-1-8 formation with eight attackers in a match against Scotland. Even so, the game finished 0-0.

4-4-1-1 formation

This formation sees four players in defence, with two playing in the centre and one full back on each side. The supporting striker acts as a link between the midfielders and the front striker.

goalkeeper

central defenders

full back

midfielders

supporting striker

front striker

3-5-2 formation

The two wing backs are used as wide attackers when their team has the ball, but they also play like full backs and drop back when their team has to defend.

wing back

4-2-3-1 formation

This formation offers a lot of flexibility in the middle of the pitch. The rear line of midfielders can move back to support the defence, while the front row can move forwards to support the lone striker.

Styles of play

Within a formation, teams can play in different ways. They may place more emphasis on defence, on holding onto the ball or looking to make quick counter attacks. These styles of play can vary during a match.

Possession and direct football

Possession football is when a team tries to hold onto the ball for as long as possible. Players choose easy, safe passes and rely on team-mates to move into space to receive the ball. The opposition is forced to chase the ball and may tire and move out of position. This can lead to defenders leaving gaps that attackers can exploit. Rather than making lots of short, intricate passes and runs, teams playing direct football look to hit a long pass, called a long ball, up the pitch. This is often aimed at a striker known as a target man.

ON THE BALL

In the 1998 World Cup, the Netherlands scored against Argentina using a long ball that looped over seven defenders before finding Dutch striker Dennis Bergkamp.

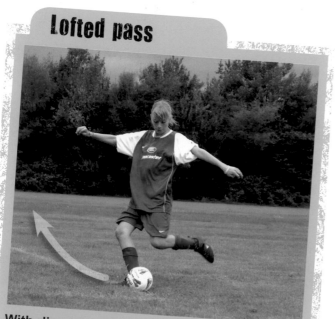

Lofted pass

With direct football, the long ball is made with the instep of the boot – this is the part of the boot where the laces are. Here, the player is leaning back slightly so that she will get plenty of height on her pass.

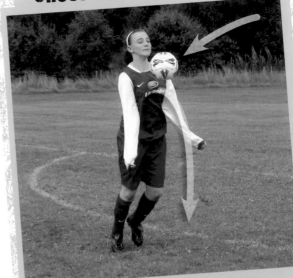

Chest control

Controlling the ball is important when receiving a long pass. This player is controlling the ball by cushioning its arrival with her chest so that the ball drops gently in front of her feet.

Counter attack

Another style of play is counter attacking. When the other side has the ball, most of the defending players withdraw into their own half. When the defending players win the ball, they launch a rapid attack, called a counter attack. Many of their opponents will be out of position, having been on the attack themselves. This can leave spaces for the attacking team to use.

Everyone has their idea of what's the 'right' style. People can like the system of play or not, but that's always going to depend on the types of players you have. The most important thing is results.

Former England manager,
Fabio Capello

Breaking free from defence

The team in yellow has just won possession of the ball and is counter attacking. The ball needs to be moved quickly away from the team's own goal and up the pitch, ahead of the opponents in blue. Team-mates look to sprint forwards to receive a pass.

rking together

...do not need to have the ball to make an impact on the ...me. Successful footballers know that their movement to ...pport team-mates with the ball is still very important.

Making and denying space

One of the most important tasks in football is making space for others. At a throw-in, for example, one attacker may run towards the team-mate who is throwing in, calling loudly for the ball. This can draw a defender forwards, pulling them out of position and creating space for another attacker to receive the throw. Alternatively, defenders can work as a unit to close down an attacker. The defender closest to the opponent will try to delay the attacker until support from team-mates arrives.

Tactics Tip

As a defender, you should know which foot your goalkeeper prefers to kick with. When you make a backpass, it should always be to that side, so that the keeper can clear with ease.

Shepherding and support

1 The defender (in blue) slows the attacker down without touching the attacker and giving away a foul.

2 The defender has moved, or shepherded the attacker away towards the side of the pitch and away from danger.

3 Even though the attacker has been able to get clear, another defender has come up in support. The attacker now has a defender in front to slow down the attack even more, and another behind to challenge him.

One-two move

1 The one-two is a simple and effective way of getting round defenders. Attacker number 1 makes a short pass to his team-mate, attacker number 2.

2 Attacker number 1 then runs behind the defender (in yellow), who has turned towards attacker number 2. Attacker number 2 then passes back to attacker number 1.

3 Attacker number 1 now has possession of the ball and has been able to get past the defender without a challenge being made.

Supporting possession

The player who has possession (control of the ball) relies on team-mates to get into good positions to receive a pass. Players should always be aware of when a team-mate gets into trouble and is under pressure from an opponent. These players can run into space and receive a short pass from their pressurised team-mate.

Backheel pass

Attacker number 1 (in blue) is being challenged by a defender (in yellow). However, attacker number 2 has got into a good position to receive a short backheel pass. This is made with the heel of the boot and is a good way of changing the direction of play very quickly.

Boosting the defence

Defence is not just for defenders. The whole side can have an important role in defending, winning the ball back from the opposing team and preventing them from scoring.

Anchors and sweepers

Some teams play with a midfield anchor who plays in front of the defence and tries to break down opposition attacks. Many other teams prefer to play the sweeper system. Here, the three or four defenders are assisted by an additional defence-minded player. As well as helping out in defence, some sweepers are also skilled at launching attacks.

Franz Beckenbauer (in white) moves past a challenger with ease. He played for West Germany from 1965–77 and turned the sweeper's role into an attacking one by bringing the ball out of defence and joining the midfield.

Tactics Tip

Even if you are an attacker, you may still need to defend. If your coach has not told you to stay upfield, look to chase down any opposition defender with the ball, and try to pressurise them into making a mistake.

Sweeper formation

Sweepers usually play slightly behind the line of defenders. From here, they can mop up any loose balls that may be heading towards the goal, or stop an opposition attack that gets past the other defenders.

sweeper

defenders

midfielders

attackers

Helping out

During a game, a team may decide to change tactics and pull back attackers to help out the defence. For example, when the opponents have a free-kick that is close to goal, the defending team's attackers often form a wall in front of the goal to stop a straightforward shot. When defending corners, a team's tallest attackers, such as England's Peter Crouch, are often brought back into their own penalty area to defend. At other times, attacking midfielders are expected to track the runs of opposing midfielders who are trying to burst through the defence.

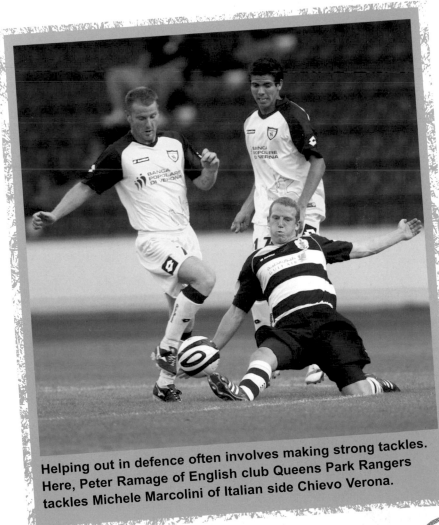

Helping out in defence often involves making strong tackles. Here, Peter Ramage of English club Queens Park Rangers tackles Michele Marcolini of Italian side Chievo Verona.

Defensive tactics

Defenders will always aim to get between the ball and their goal. Usually, they will defend using one of several marking systems, such as man-marking and zonal marking.

Marking systems

A man-marking system sees each of the defending players standing close to a particular opponent. The defenders shadow the attackers' movements, while staying between the attackers and the goal. A zonal marking system sees defending players marking areas or zones of the pitch. These areas overlap a little and move as the ball is moved around by the opposition team.

Defensive marking

These defenders (in yellow) are man-marking the attacking players (in blue). The defenders will follow the attackers closely and make sure that they are always 'goal side' – between the attackers they are marking and the goal.

Zonal marking

These defenders (in red) are using zonal marking. Each zone is shown by a black box. As an attacker with the ball enters a defender's zone, the defender moves to delay the attacker, while other defenders move towards the play to help.

defender

zone

oncoming attackers

Mixing it up

Sometimes, a team chooses to use zonal marking, but has one player man-marking a particularly dangerous opponent. By denying this important attacker time and space to perform, the team hopes to stop the opposition from scoring. Should they win the ball back, defenders have more decisions to make. Do they have time to move forwards or are opponents close to them? If they are under pressure, defenders opt for safety first, clearing the ball a long way from their goal.

Intercepting passes

1 Defenders should always be alert for an attacking team's mistake, which could lead to them winning back the ball. Here, a defender (in yellow) has spotted an obvious pass between two attacking players (in blue).

2 The defender runs up quickly and intercepts the pass. He now has the option of kicking the ball clear to safety or of launching an attack himself.

Attacking as a team

Very few goals are scored by one player acting all on their own. Most are scored as a result of skilful play from team-mates working well together.

Using the width of the pitch

Many teams use the tactic of filling the middle of the pitch with players. Other teams move players wide to the sidelines. In doing so, they can create more space between the defenders of the other team. This can lead to gaps through which attackers can run towards the goal. Alternatively, if the defenders stay quite narrow, an attacker can move down the sideline with the ball and cross it for team-mates in the penalty area.

Tactics Tip

Try not to over-complicate an attack. Do not make a long pass when a short one will do. Keep an eye out for the simplest option – it is often the best.

Creating an overlap

1 Attacker 1 (in blue) runs behind attacker 2 to create an overlap. The defender (in yellow) moves forwards to challenge attacker 2.

2 Once attacker 1 has run past the defender, attacker 2 passes to him. Attacker 1 is now clear to attack down the sideline without being challenged.

1 Attacker 1 has spotted a space between two defenders (in yellow). He aims a pass between the defenders. This pass is called a through ball.

2 Attacker 2 has spotted the through ball and runs behind the defence to collect the pass. He is now clear of the defence and can shoot at goal.

Overloads

When attacking, teams look for an overload – an area of the pitch where they have the ball and where there are more attackers than defenders. This can allow attackers to get past the defence using a one-two pass or a through ball. Good attackers also stay aware of where their team-mates are in case one of them is in a better position to score a goal.

The cutback

Sometimes, the best attacking option takes a team away from goal. The cutback is a simple attack move. It sees an attacker (shown here in blue) passing back to a team-mate who is in a better shooting position.

defender

oncoming attacker

Changing tactics

Matches do not always go according to plan and teams sometimes need to change their tactics in order to win.

Changing players

There are many reasons why a team may alter its tactics. It may suddenly go a goal up and choose to play more defensively to protect the lead. The loss of a key player to injury or a sending off is another common reason for changing the team and its tactics.

Tactics Tip

As a player, you should always think about your opponents' strengths and weaknesses. If you spot someone who can only kick with one foot, try and force that player to use their weaker foot.

Watching for a mismatch

This fast, skilful winger (in blue) gets past the opposing defender. She can now either cut in towards the goal or head for the goal line and put a cross into the opposition penalty area. If she did this repeatedly, the defending team's coach would have to think about changing tactics.

Exploiting mismatches

A team's coach watches a game closely at all times, looking for mismatches where one player is struggling repeatedly with the power, pace, height or skill of an opponent. Tactics are sometimes changed to try and cause mismatches.

One team's coach has no control over how the other team plays. They may expect their opponents to play a 4-5-1 formation only to discover the opposition going with 4-2-4. The coach may have to make changes to counter the opposition.

Choosing the wrong formation

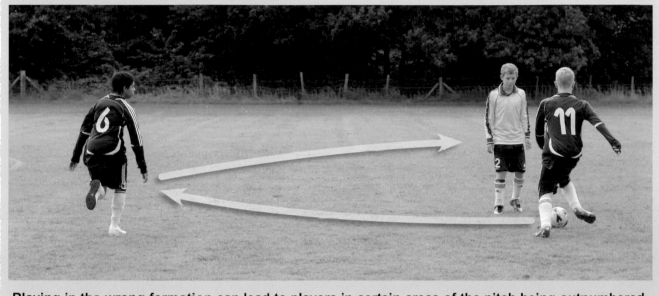

Playing in the wrong formation can lead to players in certain areas of the pitch being outnumbered by the opposition. Here, a defender (in yellow) is facing two attackers (in blue) – with quick passing, the attackers can get round the defender easily by using a simple one-two move.

In the 2010 World Cup, Slovakia's Kamil Kopunek came on as a substitute against Italy. He scored with his first touch and Slovakia went on to knock the world champions out, 3-2.

Dealing with fewer players

With a defender sent off, this team has changed formation from 4-4-2 to 4-3-1-1. A midfielder has moved back into defence, one of the team's two strikers has dropped back to play a linking role between midfield and attack, and the two wingers have moved in to play more narrowly.

Substitutions

As well as changing formations and tactics, coaches have three further tactical tools they can use. They can issue instructions from the sidelines, they can talk to players at half-time and they can change, or substitute players.

Substitute numbers

As well as the starting team of players, coaches have other players, called substitutes, sitting on the bench. The number of substitutes a coach can choose from varies from competition to competition. In the English Premier League, for example, seven players sit on the bench. From these, a coach can select up to three substitutes to bring on during a match.

ON THE BALL

During an international match against Australia in 2003, England manager Sven-Göran Eriksson substituted the entire team at half-time.

Players from the Washington Freedom (in blue) and the Philadelphia Charge (in white) compete in a WUSA women's league match in the United States. In 2001, WUSA allowed up to five substitutions during a match.

Making substitutions

Substitutions are an important tactical tool and they are not just used to replace injured players. If a team is struggling in one area of a game, the coach might make one or more substitutions to change tactics. For example, one team may bring on a defensive midfielder when it has gone a goal up, in order to defend the lead. In contrast, the losing team might bring on an extra striker or attacking midfielder to try and score. Later on in games, many substitutions involve replacing one player with another who has the same skills and abilities. The aim is to bring on a fresh player who is not tired.

An assistant referee holds up an electronic board showing the number of the player who is to be substituted. That player then has to leave the pitch, while the substitute comes on.

> *It should be 11 subs on the bench, as most squads carry a squad of 22 or 23 players. Last Saturday, we had players sitting in the stands who could have been on the bench contributing something towards the team.*

Manchester United manager,
Sir Alex Ferguson

Team spirit

Team spirit is forged on the training ground and by a team working together with a coach to achieve the same targets. However, it is also dependent on the players' determination and how committed they are to winning.

Attitude and communication

A good team attitude starts before a match. Players should listen intently to their coach's instructions, encourage team-mates and prepare well for the game. Once out on the pitch, players need to keep their eyes and ears open. Listening to team-mates' advice on positioning and warnings can be crucial, as can giving encouragement to a player who has just made a mistake.

Captain

Team captains, such as Phillipp Lahm of Germany, play an important role in keeping players' morale high. Captains should talk to and encourage their team-mates and never openly criticise them.

Goalkeeper

As well as guarding their goal, keepers must also organise their defenders. Here, the keeper is pointing out any gaps to his defenders and telling them where they should stand.

Making a comeback

The important thing when the other team is on top or when you are already one, two or three goals down is not to give up. A side with good team spirit sticks together and can sometimes come back from what looks like a desperate or impossible position. During Euro 2008, Turkey found themselves 2-0 down against the Czech Republic with just 16 minutes left. However, they did not give up and managed to score three goals in the time remaining, winning the game 3-2.

Xabi Alonso of Liverpool celebrates scoring the equalising goal during the 2005 Champions League Final. Liverpool had been 3-0 down at half-time to Italian side AC Milan, but went on to tie the game and then win on penalties.

Tactics Tip

Never ease up when your team is in the lead, even if it seems your side is far better than the opposition. It takes only a second to score a goal and many major teams have been embarrassed by a 'lesser' side fighting back and winning.

Set-piece tactics

Set-pieces are ways of restarting the game after the ball has left the pitch or a foul has occurred. Teams practise them regularly because they often lead to goals.

Throw-ins and corners

Throw-ins may seem unthreatening, but a good team can turn them into an attacking weapon. Some sides have a player who can make long throws into the opposition penalty area. Corners are awarded when a defender is the last to touch the ball before it rolls over the goal line.

Types of corner

With his team-mates standing in the penalty area, this corner kicker has a number of options. He can cut the ball back to an attacker at the front of the penalty area or he can cross the ball high into the penalty area near the goal. This high ball can curve into the penalty area, or it can curve away from the goal line to confuse the goalkeeper.

Free-kicks

Free-kicks are awarded when the opposition has committed an offence, such as a foul. Some free-kicks are taken quickly to get the ball moving and to try to catch out opponents, while others are paused over for some time. Teams will practise various free-kick moves, including passing to another team-mate who can shoot at goal from a different angle or using a dummy runner.

Side pass

1 Rather than shooting directly at goal, the side pass free-kick sees attacker 1 making a short pass to attacker 2 who is standing to one side.

2 In doing so, attacker 2 now has a clear shot at goal, without the wall of defenders (in yellow) standing in front of him.

Dummy runner

1 In this type of free-kick, attacker 1 runs up to the ball as if he is going to take the free-kick. Attacker 2 waits behind him.

2 Instead of kicking the ball, attacker 1 steps over it. Attacker 2 then runs up behind attacker 1.

3 Attacker 2 shoots, aiming away from the keeper who has been fooled by the dummy runner and has committed himself in the wrong direction.

What it takes to be...

A top coach

Jose Mourinho

Mourinho's father, Felix, was a football coach and, as a teenager, Jose watched his father's training sessions. Mourinho studied sports science in Portugal and brought a scientific attitude to training and tactics. He developed his own tactics as coach of Barcelona's B team, before enjoying success at Porto in Portugal and Chelsea in England. In 2008, he became head coach of Internazionale (Inter) in Italy and won the Italian league twice in a row, as well as the 2009 Champions League, before moving to Real Madrid in 2011.

Career path

⚽ 1992: Worked as a translator at Sporting Lisbon.

⚽ 1996: Moved to Barcelona.

⚽ 2000: Made head coach of Benfica in Portugal.

⚽ 2004: Won Champions League with Porto.

⚽ 2004: Made Chelsea manager.

⚽ 2008: Won Italian league with Inter.

⚽ 2011: Signed a four-year contract with Spanish club Real Madrid.

Mourinho won the Portuguese League twice and the Champions League when coach of Porto. He also coached Chelsea to two Premier League titles.

Glossary

coach someone who works with the players, deciding who should play and what tactics to use. They do not get involved in any business aspects of the football club.

counter attack when defenders win back possession of the ball and launch a quick attack before the opposition players can organise their defence.

full back a defender who plays mainly on the sides of the pitch.

game changers players who are so skillful that they can alter the course of a match.

heart rate the number of times your heart beats in a minute.

manager someone who oversees the running of the team, deciding which players play and what tactics to use, and gets involved in the business decisions, such as which players to buy and sell.

midfielders the players who play in the central part of the pitch.

possession football a style of play where players make short passes to each other, keeping possession of the ball.

season the continuous run of games over an entire year.

striker a team's best goal scorer and the player who usually plays nearest the opposition goal.

teamwork when players work together as a unit rather than as individuals.

wing back a midfield player who plays wide along the sides of the pitch.

Books

Football Focus: Rules of the Game by Clive Gifford (Wayland, 2012)
Inside Sport: Football by Clive Gifford (Wayland, 2007)
Sports Science: Football by Natalie Hyde (Franklin Watts, 2009)
Sporting Skills: Football by Clive Gifford (Wayland, 2008)

Websites

www.mastersport.co.uk/soccerskills.htm
Full of information on skills and tactics.
www.football-lineups.com
Contains a range of formations used.

www.thefa.com
Information on how to get involved in football, including finding your local club and the qualifications needed to coach.

Index